For my dad, Mike Corey, who was a fourteen-year-old living
in Miami Beach during the Cuban missile crisis
and who has always asked questions—S. C.

For Michiko and Jin—R. G. C.

p. 15: One brief quotation from p. 225 from PROFILES IN COURAGE by JOHN F. KENNEDY. Copyright © 1955, 1956, 1961 by John F. Kennedy. Copyright renewed © 1983, 1984, 1989 by Jacqueline Kennedy Onassis. Foreword copyright © 1964 by Robert F. Kennedy. Reprinted by permission of HarperCollins Publishers.

p. 20: Reprinted with permission from New Pittsburgh Courier, June 25, 1960.

pp. 28, 39: Reprinted with permission from The Estate of Jackie Robinson & Mrs. Rachel Robinson. Jackie Robinson™ is a trademark of The Estate of Jackie Robinson & Mrs. Rachel Robinson. http://jackierobinson.com

pp. 30, 38: Reprinted by arrangement with The Heirs to the Estate of Martin Luther King, Jr., c/o Writers House as agent for the proprietor, New York, NY. Copyright © 1963 Dr. Martin Luther King, Jr. Copyright © renewed 1991 by Coretta Scott King

p. 49, photograph: Cecil Stoughton. White House Photographs. John F. Kennedy Presidential Library and Museum, Boston

A TIME TO ACT

John F. Kennedy's Big Speech

WORDS BY Shana Corey
PICTURES BY R. Gregory Christie

North South

John F. Kennedy loved to read about history.

But history isn't just in books—it's happening all around us.

And the people who make history aren't just famous leaders or characters in stories.

They're real people, just like you.

Sometimes, they ARE you.

John (or Jack, as he was called) was the second of nine children in a big, rich family.

If you saw the Kennedys, you might think they had everything.

But take a closer look.

Jack wasn't the favorite—that was his big brother, Joe. Their father wanted Joe to grow up to be president.

No one was sure what Jack would be.

Jack didn't always do well in school.

"He is casual and disorderly . . . and can seldom locate his possessions," noted one school report.

And he was often sick.

But Jack was funny and people liked him.

When Jack was too sick to play outdoors, he read.

Jack also liked to write.

As a boy, he once wrote a letter to his father asking for a raise in his allowance.

When he got older, he thought about being a journalist and sometimes carried a notebook around to jot down his ideas.

In college, he put some of those ideas into a paper.

His father helped him publish it as a book.

Why England Slept became a bestseller.

Jack's mother taught her children the importance of giving back to one's country.

Jack took that belief seriously.

When the United States entered World War II, he joined the fight.

On August 2, 1943, an enemy ship ripped into the boat he commanded.

Jack led the survivors to safety, towing one of the injured for more than three miles by holding the man's life belt strap in his teeth.

The navy wrote to Jack's parents, praising his courage.

"Kennedy's Son Is Hero," declared *The New York Times*.

But in the water, Jack hadn't had a lot of choices.

"It was involuntary," he said. "They sunk my boat."

Jack's brother Joe also served his country.
But Joe wasn't as lucky as Jack.
A year after Jack's rescue, Joe was killed flying over the English Channel.
The family was heartbroken.
Now it was up to Jack to carry out his father's dreams for Joe.

In 1946, Jack ran for Congress.

His whole family helped.

His father gave money and advice.

His mother and sisters gave teas.

Jack wasn't a natural at public speaking at first,
but he worked hard.

He knocked on doors.

He shook hands.

And he won people over with his charm.

On November 5, 1946, twenty-nine-year-old
Jack won the election.

After six years as a congressman, Jack was elected to the Senate.

Americans loved the handsome young senator. He and his new wife, Jackie, were celebrities.

Soon after they were married, Jack had back surgery.

While he recovered, he wrote another book, with the help of his staff.

Profiles in Courage told about people who had the courage to take a stand for things they believed in, even when they weren't popular stands.

"To be courageous . . . requires no exceptional qualifications," Jack wrote. "It is an opportunity that sooner or later is presented to us all. Each man must decide for himself the course he will follow."

Which course would Jack choose?

On January 2, 1960, Jack announced that he was running for president of the United States.

Years of practice had turned him into a powerful speaker.

But not everyone thought he could win.

He was forty-two years old—younger than any president who had been elected before.

President Dwight D. Eisenhower called him "that young whippersnapper."

Eleanor Roosevelt thought Jack's father was spending too much money to help him get elected.

"MY DEAR BOY," she telegrammed. "I ONLY SAY THESE THINGS FOR YOUR OWN GOOD."

And Jack was Catholic.

Many believed the country wouldn't elect a Catholic.

"I believe in an America where religious intolerance will someday end," said Jack.

America was also in the midst of a long, hard struggle over civil rights.

Civil rights are the rights of all people to be treated fairly, without being discriminated against.

In many places, black people were not treated fairly.

In the south especially, a system called segregation kept black people apart from white people.

Even though the Supreme Court had declared it illegal, black people were not allowed to go to the same schools as white people.

They were not allowed to drink from the same water fountains or eat in the same restaurants or stay in the same hotels.

Black people couldn't always get the same jobs as white people.

And sometimes, they were kept from voting.

Many Americans—both civil rights leaders such as Dr. Martin Luther King, Jr. and others who weren't famous, even students and children—were trying to change that through peaceful protests.

"In the decade that lies ahead . . . the American Presidency will demand . . . that the President place himself in the very thick of the fight. . . . It is not enough merely to represent prevailing sentiment—We must act in the image of Abraham Lincoln," said Jack.

Just a month after Jack announced he was running for president, four college students in Greensboro, North Carolina, began a sit-in.

They sat quietly and peacefully at a "whites-only" lunch counter and waited to be served.

They were refused.

Every day, more and more students joined them.

By the end of the week, the sit-ins had spread across the south.

Some white people yelled at the protesters.

Some spit at them or threw food.

But some joined them.

And no matter what was yelled or thrown at them, the protesters sat quietly and peacefully.

Waiting to be served.

Working for change.

"The aim of the next president of the United States must be to . . . achiev[e] equal opportunity for all Americans regardless of race," said Jack. "This requires equal access to the voting booth, to the school room, and to lunch counters."

That October, Dr. Martin Luther King was arrested and sent to prison after participating in a sit-in.

His wife, Coretta Scott King, feared he would be killed.

Jack's campaign worked secretly with Georgia's governor to get Dr. King released.

Some of Jack's advisers worried this would cost him the votes of white people who didn't support civil rights.

But Jack telephoned Mrs. King. "If there is anything I can do to help, please feel free to call on me," he said.

On November 8, 1960, Jack was elected the thirty-fifth president of the United States.

He won by the slimmest of margins.

But many black people had voted for him.

Jack wanted his inauguration speech to inspire hope.

He looked to history and asked his speechwriter to study Abraham Lincoln's Gettysburg Address.

Jack wrote and rewrote.

He practiced at breakfast and even in the bathtub.

On the morning of January 20, 1961, twenty thousand people thronged the streets of Washington.

Marian Anderson sang "The Star Spangled Banner."

Robert Frost read a poem.

And finally, Jack began to speak.

"Let the word go forth . . . that the torch has been passed to a new generation of Americans . . . unwilling to witness or permit the slow undoing of those human rights to which this nation has always been committed. . . . Ask not what your country can do for you—ask what you can do for your country."

In some things, the new president acted quickly and used bold words.

He established the Peace Corps and challenged young Americans to go out into the world and work "shoulder to shoulder" with people in other countries.

The volunteers built roads and bridges, libraries and schools.

The United States and the Soviet Union were rivals, competing to be the strongest.

The Soviet Union had already sent a man into space.

Jack declared that the United States would be the first to land a man on the moon.

Less than a year later, Americans everywhere turned on their televisions and watched astronaut John Glenn lift off into space.

The space race was on!

Jack worked to keep relations with the Soviet Union peaceful.
And he traveled the world.

In Berlin, two million people cheered when he stood at the
wall that separated free West Berlin from Soviet-held East Berlin.

"Freedom is indivisible," Jack said. "When one man is
enslaved, all are not free."

But on important civil rights issues, Jack was slow to act.

He had once declared that the president must be willing to get in the "thick of the fight." But now he seemed unwilling to fight some battles.

"I would like to be patient . . . ," the famous baseball player Jackie Robinson wrote to Jack, "but patience has [cost] us years in our struggle for human dignity."

While Jack hesitated, others stepped forward and acted.

In 1961, young black and white people called Freedom Riders tried to integrate buses in the south.

Angry crowds smashed their windows.

They slashed the tires.

They set fire to the buses.

But the young people didn't give up.

That October, Dr. Martin Luther King met with Jack at the White House.

When they passed a framed copy of Abraham Lincoln's Emancipation Proclamation—the document that had freed slaves—Dr. King suggested Jack write a second Emancipation Proclamation to outlaw segregation.

But Jack worried about losing the support of those in Congress who disagreed.

So Jack didn't write a new proclamation.

He didn't take bold action.

But others were taking action.

"Oppressed people cannot remain oppressed forever," Dr. King wrote from a Birmingham jail in April 1963.

And that May, despite the danger, hundreds of black children and teenagers once again stood up and acted.

They left their classrooms in Birmingham, Alabama, and, singing songs of freedom, marched peacefully to protest segregation.

They were hauled off to jail.

But the next day, even more young people arrived to take their places.

The police blasted them off their feet with fire hoses.

They turned vicious dogs on them.

Americans—including Jack—saw the young people's courage on the news and were sickened by the violence.

On June 11, two black students applied to enroll at the University of Alabama.

Alabama's white governor pledged to block them.

Again and again, young people had shown their courage.

Jack had to act.

And finally, following in the footsteps of those who had set the course by sitting in and sending letters, marching and riding buses . . . he did.

Jack ordered the National Guard to escort the students safely into the school.

And that night, in living rooms and kitchens and diners across America . . .

. . . millions of people of all colors—children and parents and grandparents, rich people and poor people, people from the north and people from the south, people of different religions, people who'd looked the other way, and people who'd fought for change—turned on their televisions and radios and heard the president speak.

"One hundred years of delay have passed since President Lincoln freed the slaves, yet their heirs, their grandsons, are not fully free. . . .

"This Nation . . . will not be fully free until all its citizens are free. . . .

"**Now the time has come for this Nation to fulfill its promise. . . . It is a time to act.** . . . Those who do nothing are inviting shame as well as violence. I shall ask the Congress of the United States to act."

"IT WAS ONE OF THE MOST ELOQUENT PROFOUND AND
UNEQUIVOCAL PLEAS FOR JUSTICE AND THE FREEDOM OF
ALL MEN EVER MADE BY ANY PRESIDENT," telegrammed
Dr. King as soon as the speech was over.

"The Presidential statement on the color question is one of the finest declarations ever issued in the cause of human rights," wrote Jackie Robinson.

The following week, Jack sent a strong civil rights bill—one that would outlaw segregation in public places and end discrimination in jobs—to Congress.

Later that summer, on August 28, 1963, Dr. King led 250,000 people on an historic march on Washington.

People of all colors, from all over the country, came together—singing and speaking.

"I have a dream," Dr. King told the crowd.
Jack listened from the White House.
Afterward, Dr. King and the other leaders
went to meet with Jack.
Jack greeted them by repeating Dr. King's
inspiring words: "I have a dream."

President Kennedy was killed on November 22, 1963, just a few months after he addressed the nation on civil rights.

But his legacy, his words and his actions, live on.

Today, the Soviet Union no longer exists.
The wall where President Kennedy once stood has
come down.

But young Peace Corps volunteers still go out into the
world, building roads and bridges, libraries and schools.

On July 20, 1969, Kennedy's space challenge was met.

Two American astronauts, Neil Armstrong and Buzz Aldrin, walked on the moon.

"That's one small step for a man, one giant leap for mankind," said Armstrong.

And decades later, we still explore the stars.

Only now, instead of racing against one another, many countries work together in space.

And on July 2, 1964, with the help of many courageous people—people who didn't give up, who worked together over many years—the Civil Rights Act of 1964 was finally passed, making it illegal to discriminate in jobs based on the color of one's skin and providing for the integration of schools and public places.

In the fifty years since the bill was passed, there has been much progress on civil rights.

But there have been steps backward, too.

History isn't a straight line.

And it's not just words written in books, in permanent ink.

It's changing—*we're* changing it—every day.

"From here on out, you are the decision-makers," Jack once told young people. "You are the writers of history."

And so now it's your turn, to choose your course, to speak up, to act, to move the world forward—to make history.

AUTHOR'S NOTE

In 2017, John Fitzgerald Kennedy (1917–1963) would have been one hundred years old. Not so very old for someone who has been part of our national memory for more than fifty years now.

Kennedy left many lasting legacies despite his less than four years in office. The space program. The Peace Corps. But as I began researching this book, I became most interested in Kennedy's relationship with the civil rights movement.

Kennedy's own focus was foreign policy and the Cold War. But decades after his death, civil rights in America is something we're still grappling with. I believe that the more we know about the past, the better able we are to go forward in the future, and so I was interested to see how Kennedy acted and reacted. Not everyone will launch a space program. But each of us will be confronted with choices in our lives about which course we'll take, and about who we want to be.

Did John F. Kennedy misstep with civil rights? I was fascinated by the fact that with *Profiles in Courage,* Kennedy had literally written a book about leaders having the courage to stand by their beliefs even when it meant going against popular opinion. And yet, when confronted with thorny political realities himself, Kennedy seemed to hesitate.

Kennedy did take steps forward. The day of his inauguration, he ordered that the Coast Guard be integrated when he noticed the all-white troops marching past in his inauguration parade. As a congressman, he had supported fair employment, and as the president he created the President's Committee on Equal Employment Opportunity and worked to hire more and higher-ranking African Americans across government, starting with his own White House. He and his brother Robert withdrew from private clubs that didn't allow African Americans, and the Kennedy White House entertained more black guests than any previous administration.

And yet many of Kennedy's reforms might be seen as cautious and symbolic, motivated by concern for America's image as a democracy. Worried about losing the support of Congress, which was controlled by southern white conservatives, Kennedy didn't speak forcefully regarding civil rights early on or put forward comprehensive civil rights legislation. And his relationship with the leaders of the civil rights movement was complicated and at times tense. For every endorsement from African American papers, there were frustrated telegrams and letters from civil rights leaders urging him to take stronger action and reminding him that black people could not wait forever. I'm intrigued by these interactions with other historical figures. They remind me that history isn't just one thread or one person's story, but lots of threads that interact and even change each other. It's a conversation and we're part of it, if we make our voices heard. I've tried to give a taste of some of those interactions and voices here, but interested readers can also find the primary source documents for a deeper dive at jfklibrary.org.

Instead of leading on civil rights, Kennedy was carried along (not always willingly) by the people who were on the ground doing the work of creating change. But when he finally did speak up—prodded by leaders such as Dr. Martin Luther King, Jr., by photographs of the violence in the south that both sickened him personally and threatened America's image abroad, by the threat of more violence to come, and most of all by the rising demands for justice from black Americans and their allies—his address to the American people on civil rights on June 11, 1963, was a game changer. It was unequivocal and powerful. For the first time, an American president told the country that the system in place was in no way acceptable—not just politically or legally, but morally. And for much of white America, that was something new.

But change often doesn't happen overnight. Tragically, just hours after JFK's civil rights address, Medgar Evers—a civil rights leader who fought to end segregation in Mississippi—was murdered. And today our country's work is not finished.

Kennedy also echoed Dr. King in saying that this work could not wait. Words matter, and John F.

Meeting between JFK, MLK, and other civil rights leaders after Martin Luther King, Jr.'s speech and the march on Washington. (Oval Office, White House, August 28, 1963)

Kennedy's words helped change the conversation. You can view his full address at: jfklibrary.org.

Days later, on June 19, 1963, Kennedy sent strong civil rights legislation to Congress. After Kennedy's assassination, President Lyndon B. Johnson worked tirelessly to garner support for the bill and ultimately overcame political opposition, including a seventy-five-day filibuster in the Senate.

On July 2, 1964, Johnson signed the Civil Rights Act of 1964 into law. Dr. Martin Luther King was among the civil rights leaders who were there to witness it. The law guaranteed equal job opportunities and banned discrimination in hotels, restaurants, schools, and public accommodations. It was both a major step forward in the civil rights movement and a lasting part of President Kennedy's legacy as well as President Johnson's.

John F. Kennedy was president during one of the most tumultuous times in American history. I wrote this book because I think he was right in *Profiles in Courage*. Courage means speaking up and taking action, even when we're speaking up for things that may not be popular with everyone. I am thankful to all the change makers—the leaders, the children, and President Kennedy—for doing so. I also wrote this book because I wanted to know more about that part of the story, because I had—I *have*—questions.

And so I ask readers: Should leaders be at the front of change? Or is it regular citizens who create change, who start the conversation? Does the fact that Kennedy waited to act change the power of his words and actions? Or can we still applaud them? What would you have done? What *will* you do when you're faced with a similar situation? It's your story: what do *you* think?

WHO ARE SOME OF THE OTHER PEOPLE IN THIS BOOK?

Eleanor Roosevelt (1884–1962) was a wealthy white woman who became First Lady of the United States in 1933 when her husband, Franklin D. Roosevelt, was elected president. She was an advocate for the rights of women, the poor, and minorities. After her husband's death, she was appointed to the United Nations General Assembly, where she worked to draft the Universal Declaration of Human Rights. She later served on the National Advisory Committee of the Peace Corps.

Ruby Bridges (1954–) became the first African American child to integrate a southern white elementary school in 1960 at age six. She was escorted into her new school in New Orleans by her mother and US marshalls as angry mobs threatened violence outside.

The Greensboro Four were four African American freshmen at North Carolina A&T University—Ezell Blair, Jr. (now known as Jireel Khazan), Franklin McCain, Joseph McNeil, and David Richmond—who began the sit-in movement when they sat at the whites-only lunch counter in a Greensboro, North Carolina, Woolworth's on February 1, 1960.

Dr. Martin Luther King, Jr. (1929–1968) was an African American minister and a civil rights activist and leader. He led nonviolent protests, including the Montgomery bus boycott, to work for equality and desegregation through peaceful means. In 1963, he, along with other activists, organized the famous march on Washington where he gave his "I Have a Dream" speech. Dr. Martin Luther King won the Nobel Peace Prize in 1964. He was assassinated on April 4, 1968, in Memphis, Tennessee. Today we celebrate Martin Luther King Day in January as a day of service.

Coretta Scott King (1927–2006) was an African American activist, author, and civil rights leader. She was the wife of Martin Luther King, Jr. Following his death, Coretta succeeded in making her husband's birthday a national holiday. An award was named in her honor (the Coretta Scott King Award), which is presented to authors and illustrators who create excellent books about the African American experience for young people.

Jackie Robinson (1919–1972) broke the color barrier and became the first African American to play in the major leagues when he joined the Brooklyn Dodgers in 1947. He was named Rookie of the Year his first season and was inducted into the Baseball Hall of Fame in 1962. Jackie Robinson was also an activist and advocate for social change.

Marian Anderson (1897–1993) is remembered both as one of America's greatest singers and as a groundbreaker for African American performers. When the Daughters of the American Revolution refused to let her perform in Washington, DC's Constitution Hall, First Lady Eleanor Roosevelt resigned in protest, and Anderson performed instead at the Lincoln Memorial. She was also the first African American to sing at the Metropolitan Opera.

Lyndon B. Johnson (1908–1973), often referred to as LBJ, was a white man from Texas who served as vice president under John F. Kennedy. When Kennedy was assassinated, Johnson took over the office, becoming our thirty-sixth president. Using the civil rights bill that JFK created, and with the help of Attorney General Robert Kennedy (JFK's brother), LBJ fought hard and eventually succeeded in having the Civil Rights Act of 1964 passed.

FOR FURTHER READING

Bridges, Ruby. *Through My Eyes.* Scholastic Press: New York, 1999.

King, Dr. Martin Luther, Jr. *I Have a Dream,* illustrated by Kadir Nelson. Schwartz & Wade Books: New York, 2012.

Krull, Kathleen. *The Brothers Kennedy.* Simon & Schuster Books for Young Readers: New York, 2010.

Lowery, Lynda Blackmon. *Turning 15 on the Road to Freedom: My Story of the Selma Voting Rights March.* Dial Books: New York, 2015.

Pinkney, Andrea Davis. *Sit-In: How Four Friends Stood Up by Sitting Down.* Little Brown: New York, 2010.

Rappaport, Doreen. *Jack's Path of Courage: The Life of John F. Kennedy.* Disney Hyperion Books: New York, 2010.

———. *Martin's Big Words: The Life of Dr. Martin Luther King, Jr.* Hyperion Books for Children: New York, 2001.

Robinson, Sharon. *Jackie Robinson: American Hero.* Scholastic: New York, 2013.

Upadhyay, Ritu, and the editors of *Time for Kids. John F. Kennedy: The Making of a Leader.* HarperCollins Publishers: New York, 2005.

In addition to the many great books on John F. Kennedy and the civil rights movement, you can find additional material, including primary source documents, multimedia, and lesson plans, at:

http://civilrights.jfklibrary.org/Lesson-Plans/The-President-Takes-a-Stand

http://www.ducksters.com/history/civil_rights/african-american_civil_rights_movement.php

https://www.gwu.edu/~erpapers/teachinger/lesson-plans/er-and-jfk.cfm

http://www.jfklibrary.org/Exhibits/Permanent-Exhibits/The-Space-Race.aspx

SELECTED BIBLIOGRAPHY

Black, Allida June Hopkins, John Sears, Christopher Alhambra, Mary Jo Binker, Christopher Brick, John S. Emrich, Eugenia Gusev, Kristen E. Gwinn, and Bryan D. Peery (ed.). *Eleanor Roosevelt, John Kennedy, and the Election of 1960: A Project of The Eleanor Roosevelt Papers.* Model Editions Partnership: Columbia, S.C., 2003. Electronic version based on unpublished letters. https://www2.gwu.edu/~erpapers/mep/displaydoc.cfm?docid=jfk09

Bryant, Nick. *The Bystander: John F. Kennedy and the Struggle for Black Equality.* Basic Books: New York, 2006.

Dallek, Robert. *An Unfinished Life: John F. Kennedy 1917–1963.* Little Brown and Co.: Boston, 2003.

Fourth-Quarter Report from Housemaster, Papers of John F. Kennedy. Personal Papers. Early Years, 1928–1940. Correspondence, 1929–1935. http://www.jfklibrary.org/Asset-Viewer/Archives/JFKPP-001-010.aspx

Hersey, John. "Survival." *The New Yorker,* June 17, 1944, p. 31.

JFKPPP (JFK Pre-Presidential Papers). House of Representatives Files (Box 93). "Kennedy Fights for Civil Rights." Undated.

Kennedy, John F., foreword by Robert F. Kennedy. *Profiles in Courage.* HarperCollins Publishers: New York, 1955.

King, Coretta Scott. *My Life with Martin Luther King, Jr.* Holt, Rinehart, and Winston: New York, 1969, p. 196.

———. *My Life with Martin Luther King, Jr.,* revised. Henry Holt: New York, 1993.

King, Dr. Martin Luther, Jr. "Letter from a Birmingham Jail" April 16, 1963. http://www.thekingcenter.org/archive/document/letter-birmingham-city-jail-0

Prattis, P. "The Courier Questions a Presidential Hopeful: Sen. John Fitzgerald Kennedy." *Pittsburgh Courier,* June 25, 1960, B4.

Purdum, Todd S. *An Idea Whose Time Has Come: Two Presidents, Two Parties, and the Battle for the Civil Rights Act of 1964.* Henry Holt: New York, 2004.

Rieder, Jonathon. "The Day President Kennedy Embraced Civil Rights—and the Story Behind It." Atlantic.com, June 11, 2013.

QUOTES WERE DRAWN FROM THE FOLLOWING:

p. 9 "He is casual . . ." (Fourth-Quarter Report from Housemaster)

p. 11 "Kennedy's Son Is . . ." (*The New York Times,* August 20, 1943, p.1)
"It was involuntary . . ." (*The Letters of John F. Kennedy,* p. 5)

p. 15 "To be courageous . . ." (*Profiles in Courage,* p. 225)

p. 17 "that young whippersnapper" (*An Unfinished Life,* p. 302)
"My dear boy . . ." (*Eleanor Roosevelt, John Kennedy, and the Election of 1960: A Project of The Eleanor Roosevelt Papers*)
"I believe in . . ." (https://www.jfklibrary.org/Research/Research-Aids/JFK-Speeches/Houston-TX_19600912-Houston-Ministerial-Association.aspx)

p. 19 "In the decade . . ." (John F. Kennedy: "The Presidency In 1960 - National Press Club, Washington, DC," January 14, 1960. Online by Gerhard Peters and John T. Woolley, The American Presidency Project. http://www.presidency.ucsb.edu/ws/?pid=25795)

p. 20 "The aim of . . ." (*New Pittsburgh Courier,* June 25, 1960)

p. 23 "If there is . . ." (*My Life with Martin Luther King, Jr.,* p. 196)

p. 25 "Let the word . . ." (John F. Kennedy's Inaugural Address, January 20, 1961; transcript and video can be viewed at http://www.jfklibrary.org/Asset-Viewer/BqXIEM9F4024ntFl7SVAjA.aspx)

p. 26 "shoulder to shoulder" (Universal newsreels, John F. Kennedy Presidential Library and Museum, March 13, 1961)

p. 27 "Freedom is indivisible . . ." (Remarks in Berlin, June 26, 1963; transcript and video can be viewed at http://www.jfklibrary.org/Asset-Viewer/oEX2uqSQGEGIdTYgd_JL_Q.aspx)

p. 28 "thick of the . . ." (John F. Kennedy: "The Presidency In 1960 - National Press Club,

Washington, DC," January 14, 1960. Online by Gerhard Peters and John T. Woolley, The American Presidency Project. http://www.presidency.ucsb.edu/ws/?pid=25795)

"I would like . . ." (Papers of John F. Kennedy. Presidential Papers. White House Staff Files of Harris Wofford. Alphabetical File, 1956–1962. Robinson, Jackie, 1961: July 28–September 5. http://jackierobinson.com)

30 "Oppressed people cannot . . ." ("Letter from Birmingham Jail" http://www.thekingcenter.org/archive/document/letter-birmingham-city-jail-0)

36–37 "One hundred years . . ." (Papers of John F. Kennedy. President's Office Files. Speech Files. Radio and television address on civil rights, June 11, 1963. https://www.jfklibrary.org/Asset-Viewer/Archives/JFKPOF-045-005.aspx)

38 "It was one . . ." (Papers of John F. Kennedy. Presidential Papers. White House Central Subject Files. Speeches (SP). Speeches: 3–86: Radio and TV address on civil rights, June 11, 1963: Executive.

http://www.jfklibrary.org/Asset-Viewer/Archives/JFKWHCSF-0926-033.aspx)

p. 39 "The Presidential statement . . ." (Papers of John F. Kennedy. Presidential Papers. President's Office Files. Subjects. Civil rights: General, June 1963: 5–13 and John F. Kennedy Presidential Library and Museum, Boston, Massachusetts. Papers of John F. Kennedy, Presidential Papers, White House Central File, Subject File. http://www.jfklibrary.org/Asset-Viewer/fXbXxZHwaUmJqbxW_5IrQg.aspx. http://jackierobinson.com)

p. 41 "I have a . . ." (An Unfinished Life, p. 645)

p. 44 "That's one small . . ." (https://www.nasa.gov/mission_pages/apollo/apollo11.html)

p. 46 "From here on . . ." (John F. Kennedy: "Statement of Senator John F. Kennedy, Message of Senator John F. Kennedy to the Nation's New Voters," October 5, 1960. Online by Gerhard Peters and John T. Woolley, The American Presidency Project. http://www.presidency.ucsb.edu/ws/?pid=60424)

ACKNOWLEDGMENTS

Grateful acknowledgment to Alexis Bucher (Textual Reference Staff at the John F. Kennedy Presidential Library), for her assistance in finding primary source documents; to Jonathan Rieder (Professor, Barnard College, Columbia University and author of *Gospel of Freedom: Martin Luther King, Jr.'s Letter from Birmingham Jail and The Struggle That Changed a Nation* and *The Word of the Lord is Upon Me: The Righteous Performance of Martin Luther King, Jr.*), for reviewing this manuscript for historical accuracy (any mistakes that remain are my own); to Dhonielle Clayton (author, founder Cake Literary), for invaluable insight in reviewing this manuscript and working with me to broaden my own understanding of the conversation; to Off the Page (offthepageeducation.org), for information on the civil rights movement and discussing it with kids; to Vaunda Micheaux Nelson, Lynda Blackmon Lowery, and Jeff Haynes, for being early readers; to Angela Ellis Roberts, for research assistance; to my agent, Tracey Adams, at Adams Literary and my wonderful editor, Beth Terrill, at NorthSouth Books, for starting this conversation with me.